WISDOM

of

PUGS

MOSELEY ROAD INC.
International Rights and Packaging
22 Knollwood Avenue
Elmsford, NY 10523
www.moseleyroad.com

President: Sean Moore
Editor: Finn Moore
Art director and photo research: Grace Moore
Printed in China

ISBN978-1-62669-152-0

WISDOM
of
PUGS

Compiled by
Grace Moore

Moseley Road, Inc.
Elmsford, New York

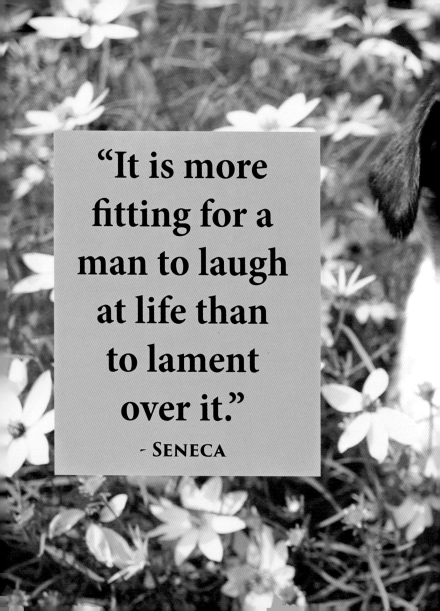

"It is more fitting for a man to laugh at life than to lament over it."

- SENECA

"Time you enjoy wasting is not wasted time."
- MARTHE TROLY- CURTIN

"Happiness is not something readymade. It comes from your own actions."

- DALAI LAMA

"Learn to let go.

That is
the key to
happiness."
- BUDDHA

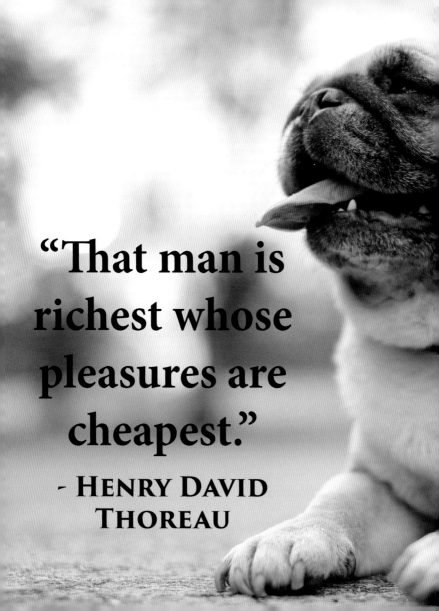

"That man is richest whose pleasures are cheapest."

- HENRY DAVID THOREAU

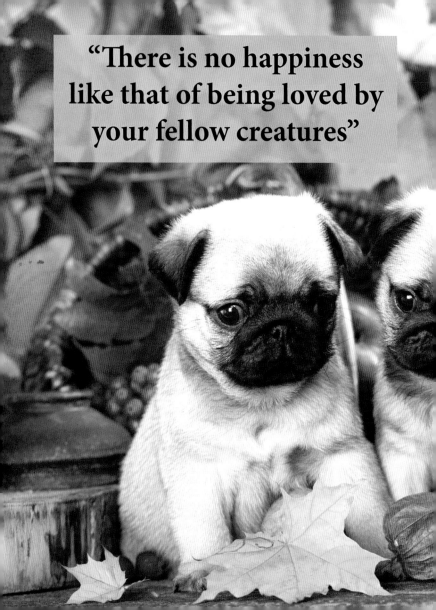

"There is no happiness
like that of being loved by
your fellow creatures"

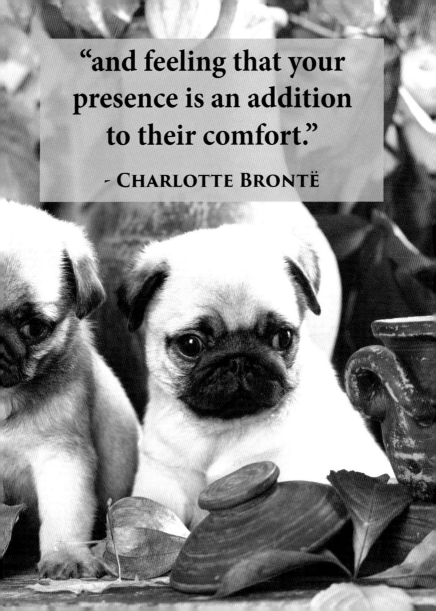

"and feeling that your presence is an addition to their comfort."

- CHARLOTTE BRONTË

"Just because you are happy it does not mean that the day is perfect but that you have looked beyond its imperfections"

- BOB MARLEY

"Happiness and the absurd are two sons of the same earth. They are inseparable."

- ALBERT CAMUS

"Once you replace negative thoughts with positive ones, you'll start having positive results."

- WILLIE NELSON

"Yesterday is not ours to recover,"

"but tomorrow is ours to win or lose."

- LYNDON B. JOHNSON

"Happiness

depends upon

ourselves."

- ARISTOTLE

"It was only a sunny smile, and little it cost in the giving, but like morning light it scattered the night and made the day worth living."

- F. SCOTT FITZGERALD

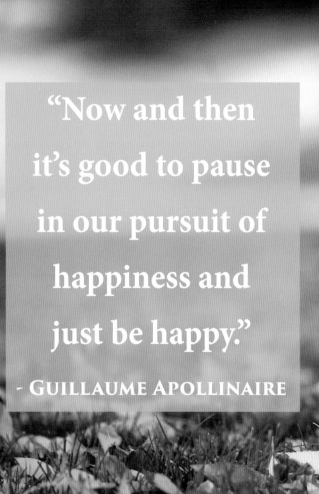

"Now and then it's good to pause in our pursuit of happiness and just be happy."

- GUILLAUME APOLLINAIRE

"There is a kind of happiness and wonder that makes you serious. It is too good to waste on jokes."

- C.S. LEWIS

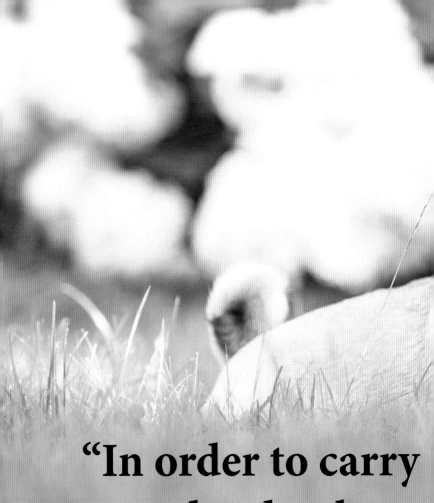

"In order to carry
must develop here

a positive action we
a positive vision."

- DALAI LAMA

"I always like to look on the optimistic side of life, but I am realistic enough to know that life is a complex matter."

- WALT DISNEY

"What sunshine is to flowers, smiles are to humanity. These are but trifles, to be sure; but scattered along life's pathway, the good they do is inconceivable."

- JOSEPH ADDISON

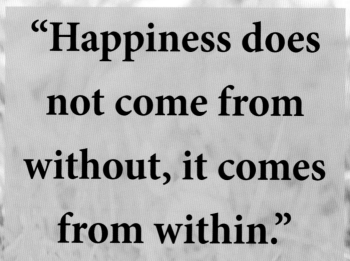

"Happiness does not come from without, it comes from within."

- HELEN KELLER

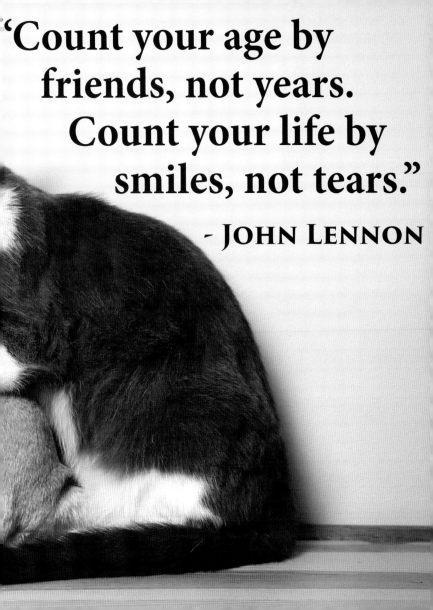

"Count your age by friends, not years. Count your life by smiles, not tears."

- JOHN LENNON

"You cannot protect yourself from sadness without protecting yourself from happiness."

- Jonathan Safran Foer

"Happiness is not a goal... it's a

by-product of a life well lived."

- ELEANOR ROOSEVELT

"The trick is in what one emphasizes. We either make ourselves miserable, or we make ourselves happy. The amount of work is the same."

- CARLOS CASTANEDA

"Happiness is a perfume you cannot pour on others without getting some on yourself."

- RALPH WALDO EMERSON

"Follow your bliss and don't be afraid, and doors will open where you didn't know they were going to be."

- JOSEPH CAMPBELL

"Attitude is a little thing that makes a big difference."

- WINSTON CHURCHILL

"The more man meditates upon good thoughts, the better will be his world and the world at large."

- CONFUCIUS

"The moments of happiness we enjoy take us by surprise.

It is not that we seize them but that they seize us."

- ASHLEY MONTAGU

"You can't make positive choices for the rest of your life without an environment that makes those choices

easy, natural, and enjoyable."

- DEEPAK CHOPRA

"Pessimism leads to weakness, optimism to power."

- WILLIAM JAMES

"With mirth and laughter let old wrinkles come."

- WILLIAM SHAKESPEARE

"The advantage of
a bad memory
is that one enjoys
several times
the same good things
for the first time."

- FRIEDRICH NIETZSCHE

"All happiness depends on courage and work."

- HONORÉ DE BALZAC

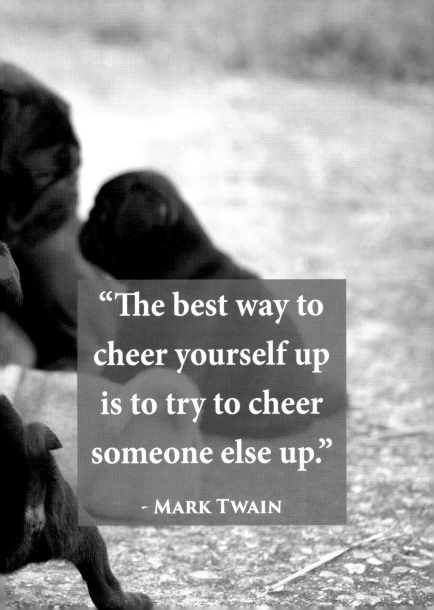

"The best way to cheer yourself up is to try to cheer someone else up."

- MARK TWAIN

"The most important thing is to enjoy your life—to be happy—it's all that matters."

- AUDREY HEPBURN

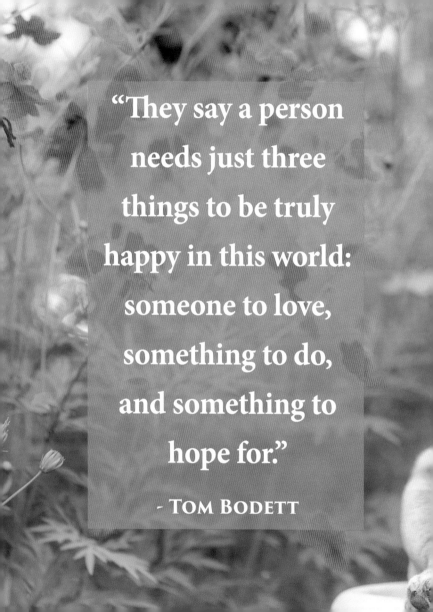

"They say a person needs just three things to be truly happy in this world: someone to love, something to do, and something to hope for."

- TOM BODETT

"Do not set aside your happiness. Do not wait to be happy in the future. The best time to be happy is always now."

- ROY T. BENNETT

"Laughter
is
poison
to
fear."

- GEORGE
R.R. MARTIN

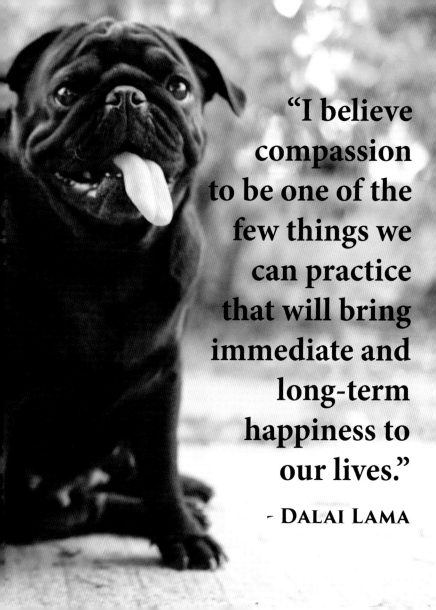

"I believe compassion to be one of the few things we can practice that will bring immediate and long-term happiness to our lives."

- DALAI LAMA

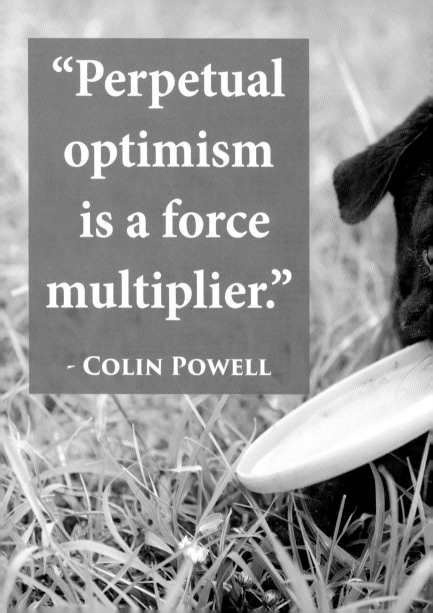

"Perpetual optimism is a force multiplier."

- COLIN POWELL

"Positive thinking will let you do everything better than negative thinking will."

- ZIG ZIGLAR

"Love is that condition in which the happiness

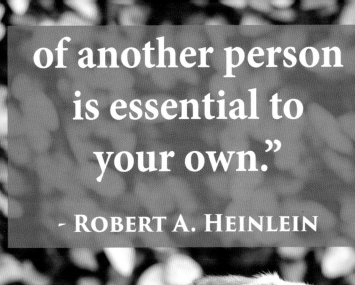

of another person
is essential to
your own."

- ROBERT A. HEINLEIN

"Happiness depends upon ourselves."

- ARISTOTLE

"Happiness consists of
living each day
as if it were
the first day
of your honeymoon
and the last day
of your vacation."

- LEO TOLSTOY

"I, not events, have the power to make me happy or unhappy today. I can choose which it shall be. Yesterday is dead, tomorrow hasn't arrived yet. I have just one day, today, and I'm going to be happy in it."

- GROUCHO MARX

"Optimism is a happiness magnet. If you stay positive, good things and good people will be drawn to you."

- Mary Lou Retton

"I'm a very
positive thinker,

"and I think that is what helps me the most in difficult moments."

- ROGER FEDERER

"In every day, there are 1,440 minutes. That means we have 1,440 daily opportunities to make a positive impact."

- LES BROWN

"Thousands of candles can be lighted from a single candle, and the life of the candle will not be shortened. Happiness never decreases by being shared."

- BUDDHA

"Happiness is when
what you think,
what you say,
and what you do
are in harmony."

- MAHATMA GANDHI

"Those who are not looking for happiness are the most likely to find it, because those who are searching forget that the surest way to be happy is to seek happiness for others."

- MARTIN LUTHER KING JR.

"True happiness is to enjoy the present, without anxious dependence upon the future, not to amuse ourselves with either hopes or fears but to rest satisfied with what we have, which is sufficient, for he that is so wants nothing. The greatest blessings of mankind are within us and within our reach. A wise man is content with his lot, whatever it may be, without wishing for what he has not."

- SENECA

"The thing that lies at the foundation of positive change, the way I see it, is service to a fellow human being."

- LEE IACOCCA

"Positive thinking is more than just a tagline. It changes the way we behave. And I firmly believe that when I am positive, it not only makes me better, but it also makes those around me better."

- HARVEY MACKAY

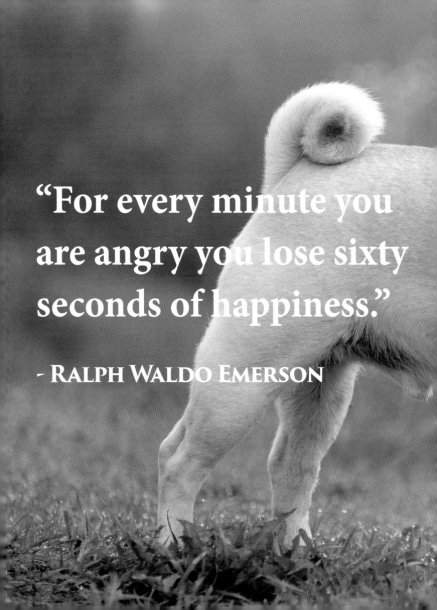

"For every minute you are angry you lose sixty seconds of happiness."

- RALPH WALDO EMERSON

"If more of us valued food
and cheer and song
above hoarded gold,
it would be
a merrier world."

- J. R. R. TOLKEIN

"There's nothing like deep breaths after laughing that hard. Nothing in the world like a sore stomach for the right reasons."

- STEPHEN CHBOSKY

"If you want happiness for an hour –
take a nap.
If you want happiness for a day –
go fishing.
If you want happiness for a year –
inherit a fortune.
If you want happiness for a lifetime –
help someone else."

CHINESE PROVERB

PICTURE CREDITS